P9-EJO-477

GREAT EXPLORATIONS

RICHARD FRANCIS BURTON

Explorer, Scholar, Spy

Serinity Young

Marshall Cavendish
Benchmark
New York

Marshall Cavendish Benchmark
99 White Plains Road
Tarrytown, NY 10591-9001
www.marshallcavendish.us

Copyright © 2007 by Marshall Cavendish Corporation
Map copyright © 2007 by Marshall Cavendish Corporation
Map by Rodica Prato

All rights reserved. No part of this book may be reproduced or utilized in any form or by any means electronic or mechanical, including photocopying, recording, or by any information storage and retrieval system, without permission from the copyright holders.

All Internet sites were available and accurate when the book was sent to press.

Library of Congress Cataloging-in-Publication Data

Young, Serinity.
Richard Francis Burton : explorer, scholar, spy / by Serinity Young.
p. cm. — (Great explorations)
Summary: "An examination of the life and journeys of the famed world explorer"—Provided by publisher.
Includes bibliographical references and index.
ISBN-13: 978-0-7614-2222-8
ISBN-10: 0-7614-2222-6
1. Burton, Richard Francis, Sir, 1821–1890—Juvenile literature.
2. Explorers—Great Britain—Biography—Juvenile literature.
3. Scholars—Great Britain—Biography—Juvenile literature. I. Title. II. Series.

G246.B8Y68 2006
910.92—dc22

2005027932

Photo research by Anne Burns Images
Cover photo: Bridgeman Art Library/Museo d'Arte Moderna di Ca Pesaro
Cover photo inset: Bridgeman Art Library/Private Collection/Stapleton Collection

The photographs in this book are used by permission and through the courtesy of: *Getty Images:* 5, 58, 73. *Corbis:* Gianni Dagli Orti, 8; Bettman, 10; Hulton Deutsch Collection, 14, 37; Historical Picture Archive, 19; Michael Maslan Historic Photographs, 45; Paul Almasy, 52; Corbis, 54; Lake County Museum, 56; Alinari Archives, 66. *Bridgeman Art Library:* Private Collection, 12, 20, 69; Yale Center for British Art, Paul Mellon Collection, 15; National Trust Photographic Library/John Hammond, 17; Andrew McIntosh Collection, 22; The Stapleton Collection, 25, 47; Christie's Images, 28, 61; Hamburger Kunsthalle, 30-31; The Fine Art Society, London, 32; Royal Geographic Society, 35; Blackburn Museum and Art Gallery, 40-41; Orleans House Gallery, 42; Archives Charmet, 59; Harris Museum and Art Gallery, 63; Trustees of the Watts Gallery, 70. *The Image Works:* Mary Evans Picture Library, 49.

Printed in China
1 3 5 6 4 2

j 910.92
B974
[B]

Contents

foreword

Richard Burton was one of the most talented and widely traveled scholar-explorers of the nineteenth century. He possessed enormous powers of physical endurance and was conspicuously brave when facing weapons of any kind, especially when he was outnumbered by his adversaries. These talents would serve him well as he traveled through some of the most dangerous parts of the world. He also possessed an astonishing memory that helped him learn almost thirty languages, and he displayed a lifelong interest in how other people lived and what they believed. He was a soldier, a writer, a scholar, a diplomat, and a spy. Even in an age of daring adventurers, few equaled him. He traveled to the Muslim holy city of Mecca—a place forbidden to non-Muslims. For a non-Muslim to be caught there meant, and continues to mean, certain death. Later, facing great physical difficulties, he discovered Lake Tanganyika in East Africa.

Richard Francis Burton combined his knowledge of diverse foreign languages and cultures with a boundless sense of adventure to leave a permanent mark on the history of exploration.

He also made some of the first translations of Asian and Middle Eastern literature, and he published richly detailed books about the places he visited and the customs of the people who lived there. He was dashing, bold, arrogant, brilliant, and brave. Because of his military and scholarly activities in Afghanistan, Pakistan, and the Middle East, the story of his exploits bears direct relevance to some of the most pressing political issues of our time.

O N E

Burton and the British Empire

Burton's life of adventure was possible because of the expansion of European colonial powers throughout the world. Burton was an Englishman who lived at the height of the British empire, a vast domain ruled by Queen Victoria from 1837 to 1901. It offered thousands of square miles of uncharted territory, ripe for adventurers seeking to access once-distant places and learn about previously foreign cultures. Burton was one of its greatest explorers, if not the most successful in terms of financial and personal satisfaction.

Though a complete believer in the superiority of the English, Burton saw much to criticize in British colonial rule, especially the isolation of British colonials from the local population. He was equally critical of the superstitions and harsh laws of the countries he explored. Such unpopular political opinions, combined with his outspoken and dominating personality, earned him enemies among his countrymen and

The mid- to late nineteenth century was defined by the reign of Queen Victoria. During her more than sixty-three years of rule, from 1837 to 1901, Great Britain vastly expanded its foreign holdings.

foreigners alike. Above all, his interest in human sexual practices shocked and fascinated his fellow countrymen, as did his unconventional views about religion. He was among the first Westerners to treat all religions as equal. For Burton all religions had their positive and negative aspects.

By the time Burton became an active participant in building Great Britain's empire, the English controlled their colonies by maintaining a distance, positioning themselves as superior to the people they ruled. In contrast, Burton reveled in the life of "the native quarter." He was a master of disguise, easily passing himself off as an Indian or a Muslim,

THE SUN NEVER SETS

The British empire traces its roots to the 1600s when it established colonies in North America and the West Indies. By the late nineteenth century, England controlled colonies and territories on every continent and ruled approximately one-quarter of the world. As the oft-repeated saying went, the sun never set on the British empire.

Great Britain's primary aim was to control particular markets, especially the lucrative trade in sugar, opium, tea, cotton, and slaves. At the same time the colonies created markets for British products such as cloth. The empire's extensive holdings and brisk trade made Britain the world's leading power. The British were able to expand and maintain their power base through their well-trained navy and the willingness of the citizens either to settle in foreign places or to work on behalf of the empire in them.

through his superior linguistic skills and because of his supreme abilities as an observer and an imitator. The British public admired this man who could transform himself into almost any member of their multi-national empire. Through his various adventures, the English were able to think of themselves as a nation of great men.

A master of disguise and a keen observer, Burton could convincingly imitate the appearance and social behavior of many of the peoples he came across in his travels.

T W O

Early Life

Richard Burton's father, Joseph Netterville Burton, was a lieutenant colonel in the British Army. His mother, Martha Baker, came from a wealthy family. They enjoyed a good standing in British society of the day. Shortly after Richard's birth on March 19, 1821, they moved from England to France. Richard was their first child, followed by a sister, Maria, born in 1823, and then in 1824, a brother, Edward.

As was customary among wealthy people in the nineteenth century, the Burton children were left mainly in the care of servants and tutors. The children had wild streaks and often bullied their caretakers. The boys especially loved playing with simple, makeshift weapons such as popguns and tin swords, and they were good at fighting with both. They also used their fists, stones, and whatever else came to hand in their frequent fights with the local French children.

Richard was particularly hotheaded and constantly in trouble, so

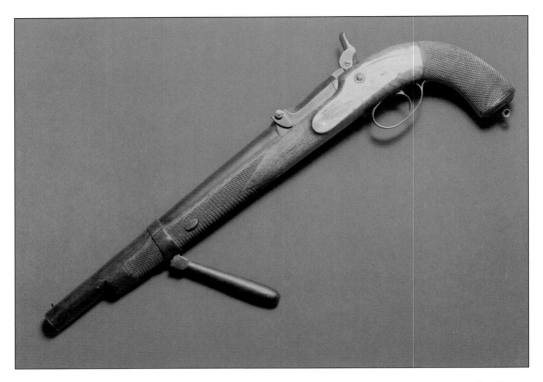

This pistol once belonged to Richard Francis Burton. His skill with weapons can be traced to his childhood, when popguns were among his favorite toys.

much so that his father grew concerned for the boy and decided to move the family back to England.

The children hated their native land, including the food, the weather, and the people. While Maria stayed at home, the boys were sent away to a boarding school whose staff members gave them little to eat and allowed violence to dominate their lives. Disagreements among students were frequent and were often settled by fistfights after class. Burton, who was proud and quick to anger, fought constantly.

An outbreak of measles in the school ended this trying period, and their father soon moved the family back to France. From then on, until the boys attended university, the Burtons lived abroad. Consequently, the children grew up as outsiders, strangers to their own homeland. This was particularly true of Richard as he grew older.

In France the children had a private tutor who added ancient Greek to their French, English, and Latin lessons. He was also an excellent fencing master, which delighted the boys, and he significantly improved their already formidable skills in swordsmanship. At the ages of nine and eleven, the brothers, already great friends, began using real foils and swords in their lessons.

The family traveled around France without setting up a permanent home. Eventually they moved to Italy, where a tutor in Italian was engaged. Learning so many languages came easily to the children and their agile, eager young minds. But despite the academic discipline, throughout this period Richard and his brother grew increasingly unmanageable. They threatened anyone, except their parents, who opposed their will.

As a cautionary measure, their father decided that they should return to England for their university education, despite the fact that they both would have preferred to join the army.

Once back in England the brothers were sent to live with different tutors to prepare them for university. The tutor assigned to Richard knew some Arabic, a language that would prove useful and valuable to Richard's future. By the time Richard arrived at Oxford he had developed a thirst for scholarship, but he found that his fellow students were not serious about their studies and he made few friends.

Meanwhile Edward was still living with his tutor and preparing for England's other great university, Cambridge. It was the first time Richard had been without his brother, and he was deeply unhappy. He would often go for walks in the woods where one day he found an encampment of Romanies, a group of itinerant or nomadic people originally from northern India. He became a frequent visitor there and even learned some of their language, also called Romany. The Romanies were

A caravan suited the often nomadic life of the Romany. It not only transported them from place to place but served as a portable home as well.

a mistrusted, often despised group, and Richard's interest in them had an enduring and rather odd influence on his life. While Burton is a common English name, it is also a Romany name, so many Englishmen came to believe that Richard Burton was of Romany descent because of his name, his dark eyes, hair, and skin, but mostly because of his incessant traveling. The pattern of moving from place to place, country to country, begun in his childhood, would continue throughout his life.

While at Oxford, he also found time to explore the mystical traditions of Judaism and what were called the occult sciences, such as astrology. These early interests proved helpful when he began to travel and study the religious traditions of India and the Middle East.

A view of Oxford University. Burton entered Trinity College, a division of the school, in 1842. He began learning Arabic and Hindustani while a student there, but his academic career was ultimately short lived.

Despite his many interests, Richard grew more disenchanted with Oxford life and started to misbehave. Matters came to a head when he attended a horse race that the university had declared off-limits to its students. He was quickly expelled. Burton's father allowed his son to follow a new direction and join the army of the East India Company, a private English trading corporation that actually ruled India. He withdrew Edward from Cambridge as well, allowing him to accept a commission in the regular army with which he was eventually sent to Ceylon, present-day Sri Lanka.

T H R E E

India

Burton sailed for India on June 18, 1842, shortly after his twenty-first birthday. Before the Suez Canal was completed in 1869, connecting the Mediterranean Sea to the Red Sea, the journey from England to India wound around Africa's Cape of Good Hope and took four months.

When Burton arrived in India the "Great Game" was at its height. This was a rivalry between the secret agents of Russia, England, Persia (now Iran), and the Ottoman empire (present-day Turkey) for political supremacy in central and western Asia. Rudyard Kipling popularized the term in his novel *Kim*, in which a young English boy born in India works as a spy. One of its characters, Colonel Creighton, was loosely based on Burton, who was one of the best British agents.

Once in India the newly minted Lieutenant Burton was eager for action. But he found the discipline of regimental life among his fellow English officers too confining. Like at boarding school and as a student

Rudyard Kipling, the author of Kim, as portrayed in this 1891 oil painting. Richard Francis Burton inspired the British author, who based one of the characters in his novel on the explorer.

at Oxford, again he felt like an outsider. Although now in a foreign country, his social and professional life was supposed to revolve around the English settlements.

Instead, with his superior language skills and dark complexion, he soon successfully took to disguising himself as an Indian and mingling with the local people. Burton was fascinated by their religions and customs, and he began his lifelong practice of making detailed notes on whatever he saw. During this time he added Hindi, Gujarati, Persian, Sanskrit, Marathi, Punjabi, Sindhi, and Jatki to his ever-growing roster of languages. He worked hard at these new tongues and dialects, sometimes studying from dawn to dusk. He also managed to find time to improve his Arabic and memorize a large part of the Qur'an or Koran, the holy book of the Muslims.

The First Afghan War

A tragic example of the Great Game was the humil-iating defeat of British troops in Afghanistan that occurred a few months before Burton arrived in India.

In their efforts to protect the northern routes into India from the Russians, the British were heavily involved in the politics of Afghanistan. A dispute between two brothers over claims to the throne gave the British a con-venient excuse to invade Afghanistan in February 1839. At first the British succeeded in occupying the capital, Kabul. However, the Afghans continued to harass British troops whenever and wherever they could. Consequently the British decided to make the long retreat to India over difficult, narrow mountain roads that were made even more treacherous by winter snows and freezing temper-atures. Sixteen thousand English and Indian troops, along with their attendants, started the long journey south. Attacked constantly, only one man survived the difficult trek.

Afghan foot soldiers wait at their post. In 1839 the British conquered Kandahar, Ghazni, and eventually the Afghan capital, Kabul. But they could not retain control of their new holdings.

Donning local attire, here a turban, Burton relied on his mastery of language, accent, and dialect to blend in with whatever local population he was seeking to move among.

At this time political power in northwestern India and central Asia was divided among various local rulers. Disputes and uprisings were frequent. At first the British were able to exploit these divisions as a way of establishing their own control of the region. It was much easier for the British to deal with local princes distracted by ongoing wars than with a strong central leader. To further their own aims and to maintain the chaotic spirit that prevailed in the region, the British often stirred up trouble between local rulers.

Imperial Russia was also increasingly interested in the region. The

British exerted their influence from the south, where they were successfully established in India. The Russians infiltrated from the north. Both sides did their best to sway local rulers in their favor, and they employed a network of spies to keep an eye on each other.

Burton was first immersed in this climate of political intrigue when he was assigned to the court of the Agha Khan Mahallati for two years. This Persian prince had recently fled to what is now Pakistan. He was also considered a Muslim holy man and had many followers, both within and outside Persia. Burton's job was to persuade the agha khan to return to Persia and wage war against the shah who ruled there. The English felt the shah was in league with the Russians and wanted him out.

Burton studied their language, dress, religion, and customs so thoroughly that he could successfully disguise himself as a Persian and pass unnoticed among them. This period marks the beginning of Burton's fascination with Islam that led to his journey to the sacred city of Mecca disguised as a pilgrim. He was particularly interested in the mystical form of Islam, called Sufism. He was one of the first Westerners to grasp its meaning and to see it as similar to forms of mysticism found in other world religions. In part, Burton's fascination with Islam may have been due to its acceptance of polygyny, marriage to more than one woman. Burton heartedly approved of this system of marriage, but he did not practice it himself.

The British often called Burton away from the agha khan's court to spy on the rest of the region. On these occasions Burton would sometimes disguise himself as a Muslim holy man, and sometimes as a merchant who would set up a stall in a local bazaar to watch what went on and gather information from the local people. Frequently, he adopted the guise of a healer, medicine being another of his many lifelong interests.

Burton enjoyed these opportunities to assume a new identity. Ever the outsider among the English, he loved being accepted into a world

An aerial view of the Muslim holy city of Mecca reveals
the Ka'bah, the windowless building that houses the sacred
Black Stone. Not even this forbidden city would prove
inaccessible to the master of disguise.

few foreigners could penetrate. Part of the thrill for him was the element of risk, for more than just fluency in the local languages or the ability to imitate local dress was required. A simple mistake regarding a specific custom, habit, or social practice, and he risked having his true identity exposed to what could become a hostile mob. In these dry regions, for example, water was so precious that it is never drunk standing up, and the name of God was invoked in different, quite specific phrases before and after drinking. Burton's ability to understand and absorb a culture stood him in good stead on these often dangerous outings.

During these spying missions, Burton's isolation was complete. There was no one to whom he could reveal his true identity as an English officer. But his inside status offered him the ideal position from which to gather intelligence. In addition to observing troop movements and picking up gossip from the bazaars, Burton surveyed the countryside, making notes about and the occasional sketch of the roads that English troops could use. He measured the distance from place to place by the steady pace of his camel. On average, camels cover 3,600 yards (3,290 meters) per hour.

The environment was often harsh in this part of the world. Burton endured temperatures that could reach 120 degrees Fahrenheit, the continuous intrusion of insects and rodents, and personal discomforts such as skin rashes, boils, and various bruises and illnesses. Burton stoically accepted all of these conditions. From early childhood he had steeled himself against pain and affliction. Without this ability, he would not have accomplished his goals nor seen things unimagined by other Europeans.

After two years at agha khan's court, Burton returned to regular military duty in Karachi, in what is now Pakistan. There, he became ill during a devastating cholera epidemic. This disease of the intestines, caused by drinking or eating contaminated water or food, is often fatal.

BURTON ON COLONIAL PRACTICE

Burton noted differences between Portuguese and British colonial policy in India. He wrote:

The Portuguese, it must be recollected, generally speaking, contented themselves with seizing the different lines of sea-coast, holding them by means of forts, stations, and armed vessels, and using them for the purpose of monopolizing the export and import trade of the interior. In the rare cases when they ventured up the country they made a point of colonizing it. We, on the contrary, have hitherto acted upon the principle of subjugating whole provinces to our sway, and such has been our success, that not only the Christian, but even the heathen, see the finger of Providence directing our onward course of conquest.

This 1842 lithograph shows a pampered young Englishman having all his whims attended to by his five Indian servants. Burton was often scornful of his countrymen and made few friends among them.

Burton was given two years of sick leave to recover, which he spent in South India. This part of India had been colonized by the Portuguese, but was now ruled by the British. It was there that Burton learned Portuguese and the South Indian languages Telugu and Toda.

Burton's time in India was coming to an end. He was scornful of his fellow Englishmen and had made many enemies among them. This did not help his military career, and he was never promoted above the rank of captain. Despite his great contribution to British knowledge of the region, his unique mastery of so many Indian languages, and his conspicuous bravery and strength of character in risking his life by traveling in hostile regions, his contributions were never fully acknowledged. His health also appeared to be severely compromised, and in 1849 he was granted additional sick leave from the army. He was so weak he had to be carried on board the ship that brought him back to England.

F O U R

Arabia

Burton recovered some of his strength on the long voyage from India and was soon settled in France. There he pursued his passion for fencing and began to write a series of remarkable books about his adventures in India. These books were highly detailed accounts of the local life, customs, and religions. As Burton took extensive notes during his travels, most of these impressions found their way into his books. Through these early publications he began to fascinate English readers with his bravery and deep knowledge of the people living in the regions they only knew as spaces on a map. Today, the explorer's accounts are viewed as valuable records of the period.

In 1852 he returned to England and offered to explore Arabia, present-day Saudi Arabia, for the Royal Geographical Society of London. At this time large sections of Arabia were still unmapped, and England wanted to know all it could to further its colonial interests in the Middle

An Arabian street scene. Burton's explorations helped further the growing knowledge of the peninsula. The life of the streets offered him yet another opportunity to observe the behavior, customs, and daily rituals of the people.

East. This latest undertaking led to one of Burton's most famous adventures—his visit to Mecca, the sacred city of Islam. Previously only a handful of Europeans had been there, and these were mostly captives, who left only brief accounts of their stay.

Burton began his incredible journey to Mecca by boarding a ship for Arabia at the Red Sea port of Suez. Once in Arabia, Burton was able to attach himself to a caravan going to Medina, the second-holiest city of Islam, and the site of the prophet Muhammad's tomb. Medina is found on one of the routes to Mecca, and pilgrims usually visit both places. The caravan traveled mostly at night to avoid the heat of the day. The travelers also formed large groups for better protection from the many bandits. Burton's caravan was attacked twice. The first time twelve men were killed. A second attack came just before they reached Mecca in September 1853.

As he often did when disguised, Burton claimed to be a man of several countries. In Arabia he said he was Pathan, a tribal people of Afghanistan, but that he had been born in India and had spent many years in Burma. Such a multinational background explained away any mistakes he might make when speaking Arabic or performing religious rituals. Since the hajj draws people from all parts of the Muslim world, he was sure to cross paths with Muslims from Afghanistan, India, Burma, and many other countries.

Another problem Burton faced in maintaining his disguise was his compulsion to take notes. This habit would immediately betray him as a Westerner. So, to deflect suspicion, he devised a system of keeping small pieces of numbered paper concealed in the palm of his hand on which he could write. He stored them in a hollowed-out copy of the Qur'an. It was a feat of incredible daring, considering that for three months he was in constant, close contact with Muslims from around the world. A single slip in language, custom, or habit might have cost him his life.

Mecca

Mecca is the center of Islamic life and the birthplace of the prophet Muhammad in 570 C.E. Wherever faithful Muslims are in the world, they face toward the city when they pray. Making a pilgrimage or hajj to the city once in their lifetime is a fundamental obligation placed on all Muslims who can afford to do so.

Even before the rise of Islam, Mecca had been a sacred site, the focus of a yearly pilgrimage to the Ka'bah, a square stone building without windows. It is

A Muslim orients the direction of his or her daily prayers to Mecca, as this man does in the 1872 oil painting Evening Prayer in the West.

enclosed by the Grand Mosque of Mecca. The Ka'bah houses the Black Stone, which is believed to have been placed in the original Ka'bah Adam built. Burton, who had the opportunity to study it closely, thought it was a meteorite. Of course, stones that fall from the sky, such as meteorites, are considered sacred by many people. Pilgrims circle the Ka'bah seven times, edging their way forward to get close enough to kiss the Black Stone.

Burton disappears into another role, this time
assuming the guise of an Arab.

With the help of Muslim friends he made along the way, his fluency in Arabic, and his knowledge of Islam, Burton succeeded in entering Mecca. He performed all the prescribed rites of a devout pilgrim, even getting to kiss the Black Stone.

He could not linger in Mecca. He had to make his way rapidly back to Egypt because he was under orders to return to his army post in India or suffer losing his commission. As he sailed for India, he began work on his justly famous, three-volume, *Personal Narrative of a Pilgrimage to El-Madinah and Meccah*, which was published in 1856. This proved to be a popular book.

Before leaving northern Africa, though, he had hatched a new plan. This time he wanted to explore parts of East Africa and to travel through Somaliland, present-day Somalia. He also hoped to enter yet another holy and forbidden Muslim city, Harar, which had never been seen by a Westerner.

FIVE

East Africa

Once back in India, Burton immediately began petitioning for leave and the financial support to make the journey through Africa. He got both. In the fall of 1854, he sailed back to Africa with two fellow officers, G. E. Herne and William Stroyan. A third companion was to meet them in Africa, but he unexpectedly died in England. This led to Burton's unfortunate acquaintance with John Hanning Speke (1827–1864), another British officer serving in India.

Speke arrived on his own in Africa, planning to explore the country and to collect plant specimens. The British authorities in Africa were not pleased with either expedition, but they suggested to Burton that he take Speke along so they would have only one expedition to worry about. First, though, the authorities decided that each of the four men should perform a separate task for the British government. Herne, and then Stroyan, was sent to investigate Berbera, an important trading

John Hanning Speke joined forces with Burton, but the combination proved less than successful.

town on the coast of Somaliland. Speke was sent to map a small river valley, and Burton was dispatched to Harar in what is now Ethiopia. Burton was quite ill several times during this journey, but he entered Harar with his usual bravado and impressed many residents with his knowledge of Islam. After a tense ten days there, where his every move was watched and as the city was in the grips of a smallpox epidemic, Burton was allowed to leave.

In the spring of 1855 the four men were united at Berbera, where they established a camp on the coast, just outside the town. They had thirty-eight men serving as guards and porters, along with camels, horses, and mules to carry their supplies. Although they had no reason to expect trouble, being well-trained military men they posted guards who were relieved at regular intervals throughout the night. On April 18, a small boat arrived bearing a group of Somalis who wanted to join the expedition. Burton was in a gracious mood and offered the captain and his crew dinner, which delayed the departure of the Somalis until the next morning. They anchored for the night about a mile offshore, a move that ended up saving Burton's life.

At around 2:00 a.m. local tribesmen attacked the camp. In the panic that ensued, all but two of the thirty-eight men working for the Englishmen fled. Burton grabbed his sword and slashed at whatever moved. Speke and Herne had their revolvers and were good shots but soon ran out of bullets and had no time to reload. They used their guns as clubs instead, but it soon became evident that they were outnumbered and had to flee. Burton thought he saw Stroyan lying on the ground and tried to fight his way toward him. It was then that one of the attackers thrust a javelin into Burton's cheek, knocking out four of his teeth. Despite the wound, Burton fought his way from the campsite and collapsed in the underbrush.

Herne, meanwhile, had made his way through the attackers and swam out to the Somali boat. Speke was not so fortunate. He had been

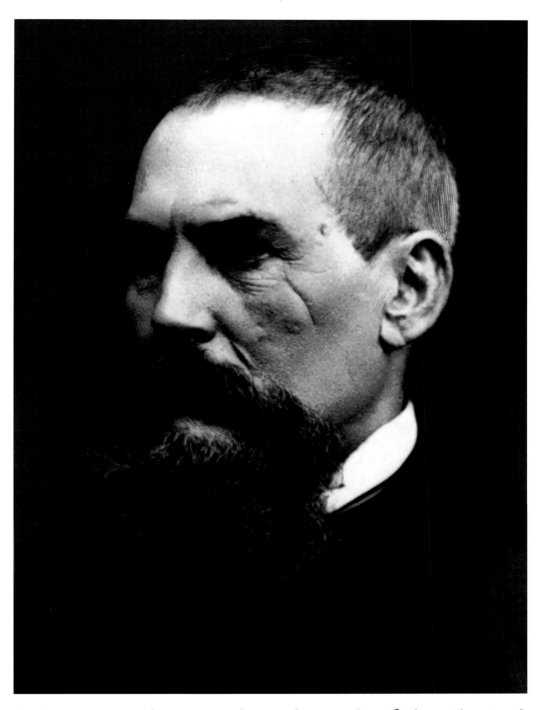

Burton's 1855 expedition turned out to be a crashing failure. The attack on the camp scarred not only his face but his reputation as well.

captured, had his hands tied behind his back, and was repeatedly beaten and stabbed. In desperation he managed to free his hands, get to his feet, and run for his life. By then the Somalis moored offshore had sent out rescue boats to try to retrieve the Englishmen. First they found Burton and then Speke. Least fortunate of all was Stroyan, whose dead and mutilated body they found at the abandoned campsite.

Speke and Burton were so badly wounded, they were sent home to England to recover. Once there, Burton did not receive a hero's welcome. Instead, full responsibility for the incident was placed on his shoulders, an unfair charge as all four Englishmen had made a brave defense in the face of an overwhelming number of attackers. Herne openly stated that even if all the attendants had stayed and fought, they still would have been overcome. Despite the words of those who spoke in his favor, Burton's reputation was badly damaged. The British considered the defeat of four English officers and the murder of one by local people to be a complete disgrace. Between this and the English preoccupation with the Crimean War, Burton's success in reaching the forbidden city of Harar was all but forgotten.

S I X

The Crimean War

While Burton was in Africa, the Great Game continued. The rivalry between Great Britain and Russia extended to other parts of the Asian continent as well. In October 1853 Russia and the Ottoman empire went to war over a border dispute. England supported the Ottoman empire to prevent Russia from expanding its power into central Asia and beyond, into India. On the English side, the war was poorly run. Political intrigue, bad military decisions, and petty conflicts among commanders spelled disaster for the British troops. Burton recovered rapidly from his African wounds and was granted leave to go to Turkey, though once there he could not get an army commission. The men of the regular British Army looked down on the men of the East India Company army despite the fact that its officers had recent combat experience, while most of the regular British forces did not.

Burton finally got a commission with General W. F. Beatson who

"Into the Valley of Death"

In his famous poem of 1855, "The Charge of the Light Brigade," the English poet Alfred Tennyson immortalized the appalling sacrifice made of young men by the generals who sent them to their deaths in a hopeless cavalry charge against Russian cannons. The poem begins

Half a league, half a
    league,
Half a league onward,
All in the valley of Death
Rode the six hundred.
"Forward, the Light
    Brigade!
Charge for the guns!" he
    said:
Into the valley of Death
Rode the six hundred.

"Forward, the Light
    Brigade!"
Was there a man dis-
    mayed?
Not though the soldier
    knew

Some one had blundered:
Theirs not to make reply,
Theirs not to reason why,
Theirs but to do and die:
Into the valley of Death
Rode the six hundred.

Cannon to right of them,
Cannon to left of them,
Cannon in front of them
Volleyed and thundered;
Stormed at with shot and
    shell,
Boldly they rode and well,
Into the jaws of Death,
Into the mouth of Hell
Rode the six hundred.

While the British lost more than 20,000 soldiers in the
Crimean War, the 157 lives claimed that day in October
1854 struck a chord with those following the conflict on the
home front. Of the event, Prime Minister Benjamin Disraeli
said, "A feat of chivalry, fiery with consummate courage,
and bright with flashing courage."

The marriage portraits of Isabel Arundell
and Richard Francis Burton.

commanded an unruly group of irregular soldiers. Before Burton joined
the unit, it had been subject to military and civil criticisms, and he was
soon actively engaged in defending the group's reputation. In the end,
General Beatson was removed from duty, and Burton resigned in
protest. Burton and Beatson returned to London where Beatson pressed
his case for defamation of character in court. Burton testified at his
trial, once more inviting public attention and making more enemies.
General Beatson was vindicated, but Burton's reputation was only further damaged. He had become something of a scandalous figure in
polite society.

Burton Takes a Wife

Isabel Arundell came from a prominent Catholic family, which was not an advantage in predominately Protestant England. A great beauty, she was fascinated by everything Asian and Middle Eastern, and she, like Burton, visited Romany encampments near her home. Her family heartily disapproved of the match with Burton: he was scandalous, not Catholic, and had few prospects of success. They completely opposed the marriage and looked on Burton's departure for Africa with a measure of relief.

While in England, Burton began seeing a young woman, Isabel Arundell, on a daily basis. They had met four years earlier but she had not impressed him then. This time, within two weeks, he proposed and she accepted. Despite the engagement, he soon left for three years of additional exploration in Africa.

SEVEN

The Lakes of East Africa

Arriving in Africa, Burton was inspired with a great ambition—to find the source of the Nile River. This desire led to one of his best known adventures. The Nile is the longest river in the world. It flows north for about 4,160 miles (6,695 kilometers) from east-central Africa and through Egypt before it empties into the Mediterranean Sea. For centuries people speculated about the location of its source. As far back as the second century, the Egyptian geographer Ptolemy believed that it flowed out of lakes in Africa. The twelfth-century Arabian geographer al-Idrīsī held the same notion. The existence of these lakes remained a matter of speculation, though, as no European had traveled into these unmapped parts of Africa and survived to tell the tale.

Burton believed that the lakes existed and that they were the true source of the Nile. He knew that if he could establish this, it would prove to be one of his greatest achievements. He also knew that the

44

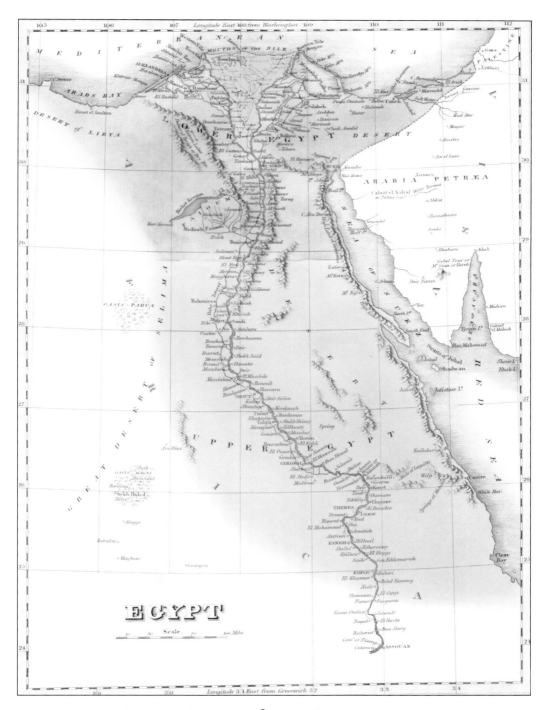

Locating the actual source of the Nile River proved an elusive challenge for many explorers of eastern Africa.

Royal Geographical Society was too conservative to fund an expedition to find the Nile's source based solely on speculation or guesswork. He misled them by saying he wanted to find an inland African lake described to him by Arab traders. The society agreed to fund that venture, and he was given two years leave from the army in which to do it. It would be a journey of staggering hardships and enduring controversy. Burton's first mistake was to invite John Hanning Speke, one of the survivors of the attack in Somaliland, to come along.

From what Speke later said and wrote, it seems clear that he already hated Burton from their previous African adventure. But he masked his feelings, even pretending to be Burton's friend. Such a dubious partnership could not and did not end well.

Burton and Speke were very different individuals. Burton was brash, arrogant, passionate, and often thoughtless. Speke was ambitious, cautious, and calculating, with a cruel streak toward men and animals. In another setting, one free from earlier resentments, these two men might have complemented each other. However, during their first African expedition, Burton had thoughtlessly rewritten Speke's journal, which he included in his own published account, *First Footsteps in East Africa*. Speke was enraged but kept his feelings hidden from Burton.

Another significant difference between the two men was evident in their attitudes toward the local people. Burton was always eager to wear local clothing as soon as possible, while Speke absolutely refused to do so. For Speke to dress like a local person was to lower himself as an Englishman. Burton was also always eager to learn all he could about the local people, including their languages. Speke had no such interests and never learned more than a few words of Swahili or Hindustani. Burton's friendly, even respectful attitude toward local people arose, in part, from his alienation from English society. Speke's aloofness and disdain for native life was quite common among Englishmen

FIRST FOOTSTEPS

IN

EAST AFRICA;

OR,

AN EXPLORATION OF HARAR.

BY

RICHARD F. BURTON,

BOMBAY ARMY,

AUTHOR OF "PERSONAL NARRATIVE OF A PILGRIMAGE TO EL-MEDINAH AND MECCAH."

LONDON:
LONGMAN, BROWN, GREEN, AND LONGMANS.
1856.

The title page to Burton's 1856 work First Footsteps in East Africa. The accompanying illustration shows a view of the walled Muslim holy city of Harar, reflecting the book's subtitle, Or, An Exploration of Harar.

of his time. This was one of the many aspects of English life that Burton never really understood. His inability to comprehend the motives and habits of his fellow countrymen had already damaged his public reputation, and it would continue to do so.

It is difficult to sort out exactly what happened on this momentous journey into unfamiliar and dangerous territory, but Burton and Speke eventually became lasting enemies. Both men endured unbelievable hardships and showed great personal courage, but clearly, the endless problems that beset the expedition wore away at them.

Burton was thirty-five and Speke twenty-nine years old when they sailed for Africa in the fall of 1856. Burton had hoped that they would be joined by other Westerners who had some experience in Africa, but this was not to be. He and Speke were the only Europeans on this expedition. To prepare, the first thing Burton did was to learn Swahili, the most common language of East Africa.

The expedition set off for the unmapped rain forests of what is now Kenya and Tanzania on June 27, 1857. Shortly after leaving, both Speke and Burton became ill with malaria, a disease caused by the bite of infected mosquitoes. Its symptoms include recurring fevers and chills that make a person too weak to even walk. For most of the journey, Burton and Speke were so ill with this disease or other tropical ailments that they had to be carried. The small party of thirty-six porters and thirty pack animals was barely sufficient to carry enough supplies for the expedition. The path they followed was through fairly thick rain forest, a route used by Arab slave traders and thus well known to the porters. Burton and Speke, however, were the first Europeans to take this route and come back alive.

Bad luck continued to follow them as porters began to steal their supplies and to desert soon after they started. Burton called for a long rest stop at Tabora, an Arab trading center, about 600 miles (966 kilometers) inland. There he recovered his strength, gave the porters a rest, and hired additional ones. Slowly the conflict between Burton and Speke began to emerge. Tensions were increased by Burton's formidable linguistic skills and Speke's complete inability to communicate in Arabic or any African language. Burton talked with locals and gathered

John Hanning Speke's injured companion, James Grant, is shown being carried by native porters during Speke's second African expedition.

the information he needed to make any necessary decisions. Speke resented his colleague's leadership abilities. Additionally, they were both suffering from eye inflammations that dimmed their vision. Still, after a few months they pushed on. Neither man can be accused of lacking fortitude or bravery.

On February 13, 1858, Burton almost turned away in disappointment when he saw a body of water in the distance. But he soon realized he had come across something of unparalleled importance—Lake Tanganyika. Remarkably, the ancient geographers had been right. Burton thought he had found the source of the Nile River. Burton described what he saw as follows:

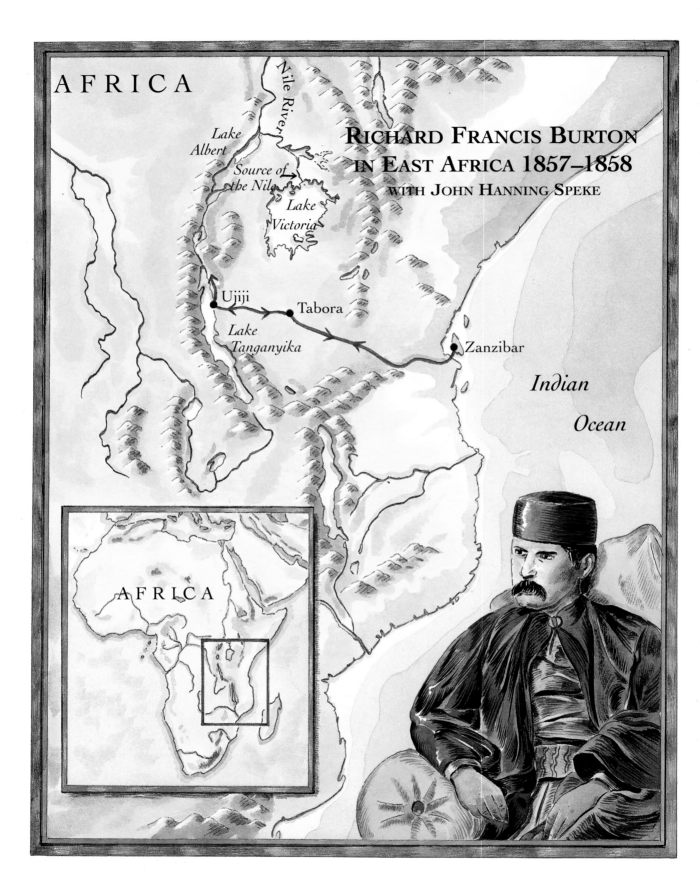

We halted for a few minutes upon the summit. "What is that streak of light which lies below?" I inquired of Seedy Bombay [a guard]. "I am of opinion," quoth Bombay, "that that is the water." I gazed in dismay; the remains of my blindness, the veil of trees, and a broad ray of sunshine illuminating but one reach of the Lake, had shrunk its fair proportions. Somewhat prematurely I began to lament my folly in having risked life and lost health for so poor a prize, to cure Arab exaggeration, and to propose an immediate return, with the view of exploring the Nyanza, or Northern Lake. Advancing, however, a few yards, the whole scene suddenly burst upon my view, filling me with admiration, wonder, and delight.

By this time Burton was so ill he could hardly move, and Speke was practically blind and soon to be almost deaf. With some effort, however, they were able to get their hands on two canoes, which they used to make some preliminary explorations of the lake.

Their health continued to fail when, on May 22, 1858, a caravan bringing additional supplies joined them. A few days later Burton started the march to the coast, stopping to rest at Kazeh, another Arab trading center. There he learned of another lake lying to the north and decided to send Speke, who was feeling better, to look for it. Obviously, Burton did not think it was going to be an important discovery, and he was glad to be rid of Speke for a few weeks.

When Speke reached the large body of water, he named it Lake Victoria after the English queen. Ironically, his vision was still so poor that

Burton and Speke were the first Europeans to reach the shores of Lake Tanganyika. Speke went on to name Lake Victoria, which he thought was the source of the Nile River. Burton would question Speke's discovery, and the true location of the river's source proved a much-debated point of contention between the two competitive explorers.

THE LAKES THEY DISCOVERED

Victoria and Tanganyika are huge lakes. Lake Tanganyika is the longest freshwater lake in the world (400 miles or 644 kilometers) and the second deepest (4,700 feet or 1,433 meters). It is 445 miles (716 kilometers) wide. Lake Victoria is the largest lake in Africa and the second-largest freshwater lake in the world. It is 255 miles (362 kilometers) long, 155 miles (249 kilometers) wide, and 250 feet (76 meters) deep.

A boulder balances on a rocky island in Lake Victoria. Of the many sights Burton personally witnessed in Africa, the world's second-largest freshwater lake was not one of them.

as he approached the lake, he could only see it as a blur. Burton, on the other hand, believing he had accomplished his goal by finding the source of the Nile at Lake Tanganyika, never saw Lake Victoria.

Burton's and Speke's accounts of what occurred during this expedition wildly contradict each other, and their competing versions were the subject of much debate when they separately returned to England. Without having explored the lake and with no substantial evidence to support the notion, Speke was convinced that Lake Victoria was the source of the Nile. He turned out to be right, even though his second expedition of 1860 still failed to support the assertion. On his second journey to this region Speke did not even see Lake Victoria, though he camped for five months within 8 miles (13 kilometers) of it. When he began to travel again, north to Egypt, he cut across country to shorten the journey. Coming upon a river he assumed it flowed north out of Lake Victoria and eventually became the Nile. Again, he was right, but his opinion was based on guesses, not on a systematic exploration of the lake and the river.

Speke got back to England before Burton and immediately began to promote his discovery. Speke quickly became the hero of the day, eclipsing Burton and his accomplishments. Burton described his shock when he reached London in May 1859: "My companion now stood forth in his true colors, an angry rival."

To make matters worse, Speke became involved with Burton's enemies in London and was at the center of a campaign to slander Burton. Partly under the influence of others, Speke took credit for the entire Africa expedition, putting himself at the center of the action and portraying himself as the one who made all the decisions. He also accused Burton of claiming discoveries that he, Speke, had made. The smear campaign was so successful that even before Burton had returned to England Speke was given command and financing for an expedition to return to Africa and further explore Lake Victoria. Burton eventually

John Hanning Speke and James Grant report on their expedition to find the source of the Nile during an address to the Royal Geographical Society in London.

proposed a second expedition, to be led by him, which would meet up with Speke's near the lake. He was flatly refused.

Within a year Burton completed *The Lake Regions of Central Africa*, describing the expedition and his discovery of Lake Tanganyika. The attacks on his reputation were compounded by the continuing refusal of Isabel's family to allow her to marry him. He needed a change and a new place to explore. So in April 1860 Burton sailed for the United States.

EIGHT

The Life of a Diplomat

Burton traveled first through the American South, but he soon headed west by stagecoach from Saint Joseph, Missouri. He had added Salt Lake City, Utah, to the list of the holy cities that he wanted to visit and had begun to study the Mormons. Though persecuted in the United States, mainly for their practice of polygamy, Burton wrote a sympathetic book, *City of the Saints*, about them. His sympathy was a characteristic of Burton's lifelong interest in different religious beliefs. While in Salt Lake City, Burton met the head of the church, Brigham Young, who made a favorable impression on the explorer, and wrote about him in his book on the Mormons.

While in the United States, Burton also studied the Native American tribes he met along his route. He was even hoping to fight them and was disappointed when this never happened. On his way to San Francisco, though, he did come across a rest house that had been attacked so

THE MORMONS

The Mormons are members of the Church of Jesus Christ of Latter-day Saints, a religious group founded by Joseph Smith (1805–1844) in 1830 in Fayette, New York. Persecution continually drove them ever farther west until Brigham Young (1801–1877) led them to the valley of the Great Salt Lake where he founded Salt Lake City as the center of their community.

Brigham Young escaped the violence and oppression he and his fellow Mormons experienced in the East and Midwest for the peace and solitude of Salt Lake City, the community he founded. He and his followers proved a major force in the settling of the West.

recently that dead bodies were still lying about unburied. From California, Burton sailed down the coast to Panama where he changed to a ship bound for England. His health and spirits were fully restored, and he was determined to marry Isabel.

Upon his return to England, Burton found that Isabel's mother still vehemently opposed the marriage. Isabel showed her devotion to Burton by running away from home so the two could marry. Once they were wed, her mother realized there was nothing she could do and finally accepted the couple. Now there was the problem of how Burton was to earn a living. When the army in India was reorganized, Burton had been dropped from its rolls, and the income from his writings was not sufficient to support a wife.

Through his social contacts, and with Isabel's help, in March 1861 Burton began his career as a British diplomat. Isabel persistently searched out diplomatic positions for her husband, a practice that did not cease until his death. They were often separated, as she sometimes stayed in England when he assumed a post, or he sent her home to take care of business matters. Despite the periods spent apart, theirs was a happy marriage.

His first post was as consul to the small island of Fernando Po, a place plagued by malaria in the Bight of Biafra, a bay on the Nigerian coastline. The climate was deadly to the English and the location so isolated there was no possibility of Isabel joining him there. It did, however, give Burton the opportunity to explore western Africa, about which he eventually wrote two books.

After sixteen months on the job, Burton was granted four months of leave. When it was time to return to Fernando Po, Burton allowed Isabel to travel with him as far as Teneriffe, one of the Canary Islands off the northwestern coast of Africa. There she set up house so that she could be closer to him while he was posted at Fernando Po. The Burtons took their time getting there, stopping off at interesting places along the

ISABEL ARUNDELL

Burton's wife lived from 1831 to 1896. His life was greatly influenced by her. Many said that her impact on her husband was negative, but she remained his most loyal supporter. She worked hard at getting his books published and at securing him government jobs. After his death, she was severely criticized for burning many of his papers, manuscripts, and journals.

Isabel Burton shown in a photograph from the late 1860s. Destroying her late husband's writings and papers provoked the ire of many scholars and students of history.

way. This was to be the pattern throughout Burton's diplomatic career. He took an enormous amount of time to reach his posts, as his restless adventurer's spirit continually compelled him to stop and explore new places.

In August 1863 Burton was appointed commissioner to Dahomey, a major kingdom in West Africa. His assignment was to convince the king to stop the slave trade, to release some Christian captives, and not to perform any human sacrifices while Burton was visiting. In this he was more or less successful. But what drew his attention the most were the female bodyguards of the king and the women serving in his army. Burton's book about his time in Dahomey discusses them at length, calling them Amazons.

Meanwhile Speke had completed his second expedition to the region around Lake Victoria. Although he never actually reached the lake, he

A Dahomey king is shown surrounded by his court and guards, in an 1892 engraving based on a photograph from the era.

published an account of the journey, *Journal of the Discovery of the Source of the Nile*, saying he had proved it to be the source of the Nile by floating out of the lake and onto the Nile to Egypt. Several statements made in the book raised doubts about Speke's abilities as a geographer and surveyor and cast Burton's arguments in a more favorable light. Eventually, a debate between Speke and Burton on the source of the Nile was scheduled in London in September 1864. On the first night, other topics were argued while Burton and Speke sat on the stage. After a while, Speke just got up and left. The next day, while Burton sat waiting for Speke to appear and for the debate to begin, he was informed that Speke had accidentally or purposely shot and killed himself while out hunting. This tragic event further clouded the facts surrounding the first expedition. If Speke had committed suicide, did he take his own life because he could not face Burton? The question remains unanswered.

Isabel had accompanied her husband to England, where she made repeated visits to the Foreign Office to get Burton another job. In 1864 officials named him consul at Santos in Brazil, an assignment on which Isabel could accompany him. For the first time, the two would be sharing their own household. Once they arrived, Burton immediately set off to explore the countryside. He also wrote books about the region and performed his consular duties as best he could.

In 1868, at the age of forty-seven, Burton became seriously ill and extremely depressed about being a minor government official in such an out-of-the-way place. The accomplishments of his youth and young manhood had promised greater financial and professional success than he had actually achieved. He applied for leave and sent Isabel to England to secure him another post. While she was away, Burton spent his time traveling extensively throughout Brazil, Argentina, and Paraguay.

In England, Isabel managed to get Burton appointed consul at Damascus, Syria, in 1869. They were both delighted at the development—he, for the chance to return to his beloved Middle East, and she,

Damascus, the capital of Syria, proved to be the Burtons' destination in 1869. For Burton, it marked a return to the Middle East, a region he had described to his wife and which she longed to see.

for finally seeing the lands he spoke and wrote about with such enthusiasm. But there were objections to his appointment, both among the English and the Turks who then ruled the region. These were signs of trouble to come that Burton either did not see or chose to ignore. He was confident that he could handle the situation.

As usual, Burton took his time reaching Syria, stopping in Europe to do some touring and to see old friends. He was unaware of the charged situation that awaited him and greatly underestimated his enemies in the Middle East who had already set out to destroy his career. Burton was walking into a tense and complex political situation in which many different nationalities and factions struggled for power in the region. Several prominent people did not want him to further complicate the situation.

For one, the British ambassador at Constantinople, Sir Henry Elliot, was worried about Burton's appointment because some Muslims believed he had insulted Islam by sneaking into the holy city of Mecca. This was not necessarily true. Many Muslims respected Burton for his scholarship and for the respect he showed to Islam. Elliot could have been a great help to Burton, but he was suspicious of Burton's every action and undermined him whenever he could. Throughout this period of Burton's life, Elliot maintained the appearance of being a friend to the Burtons. To their harm, the Burtons never doubted the sincerity of that friendship.

Burton proceeded in his usual manner when he arrived at any new post—he immediately set off to explore the region. It was part of his job to be in contact with the many different ethnic and religious groups living in the region, and he continued to travel widely during his entire stay. But his long absences only fueled his enemies' critical assessment of his performance. Given that the Great Game was still in full sway, some suspected Burton of spying and of plotting political coups.

Rasid 'Ali Pasha, the viceroy of Syria, was one such enemy. He was

A view of the interior of the Grand Mosque in Damascus,
painted shortly after Burton was removed from his post
there and returned to England. Though a city with a sizable
Muslim population, Damascus was a crossroad of
various faiths and cultures.

convinced that Burton's explorations were politically motivated. Of course, given Burton's background as a spy in the army of the East India Company, this was not an ungrounded suspicion. Isabel was also slandered, and rumors spread that she acted like a princess and treated the local people cruelly.

Damascus itself was a city splintered by many different religions and races. There were various groups of Muslims, Jews, and Christians. Western missionaries were also active in the city and the region, adding to the complexity. Religiously motivated riots in 1860 had left two thousand people dead. More trouble was expected as several nations continued to compete for dominance in the region.

Burton successfully navigated these various factions and their competing interests until 1870, when on a trip to Nazareth a Coptic Christian entered Isabel's tent. Thinking he was a thief, her servants beat him. This developed into a pitched battle with the Greek majority of the town, during which Burton fired his gun once into the air. The incident led to formal charges being brought against Burton, who the Greek community accused of entering and damaging their church and then shooting a priest. Additional incidents occurred, and tensions mounted. In such an unstable region, the truth behind any of these events was often hard to decipher.

In the end, Burton was recalled to England. The Burtons had lived in an extravagant style, and they returned completely broke. It was clear to both of them that Burton's career had been permanently damaged. Undaunted, Isabel set about getting him a new, if lesser, position. He was soon named consul to Trieste, a port city on the Adriatic Sea then under the control of the Austro-Hungarian empire.

NINE

The Translator

After the usual leisurely journey, Burton took up his post in Trieste in 1872. Also, as was his pattern, he promptly began to make frequent trips into the surrounding area.

By then, Burton had written twenty-three books, but he had not made much money from them. With his working knowledge of twenty-nine languages and nearly a dozen dialects, he decided to become a translator and introduce Eastern texts to an English-reading audience.

Although he made many more journeys, one to India and several to the Middle East, Burton turned more and more to his writing. His final books bear the mark of this increased attention. They are better written, more polished, and more thoughtful than his earlier works. He usually worked on more than one book at time, and for this purpose he liked to have a different desk for each project. Fortunately for him,

This photograph of Trieste's Miramar Castle was taken in the 1870s, the time the famed explorer was living in the area.

the house in Trieste was large enough to hold his many desks, books, manuscripts, and notes.

By 1883 he had begun to decline physically and was forced to live a less active life. All of his energy was now focused on his writing and translating. One of his projects was to organize the notes he had collected over the years on *The Arabian Nights*.

Burton had begun translating *The Arabian Nights* as early as the 1850s, and he had continued working on the project bit by bit for more than thirty years. In 1885 he finally published the stories under a typically verbose nineteenth-century title: *A Plain and Literal Translation of the Arabian Nights' Entertainments, Now Entitled The Book of the Thousand Nights and a Night.* It consisted of ten volumes and a six-volume supplement. A financial, literary, and critical success, the publication yielded more money than all of Burton's other books combined.

Also in 1885, in recognition of his services to the British government, Burton was knighted. From then on, he was addressed as Sir Richard Burton, a knight commander of the Order of Saint Michael and Saint George.

Burton's life of adventure, and then success and honor, was drawing to a close. On October 20, 1890, Burton died in the early morning. Isabel could not accept the fact that he was dead until sixteen hours later. In the meantime she frantically sent for a priest to give him the final Catholic sacrament of extreme unction. She had spent most of her married life trying to convert Burton to Catholicism. Now that he was dead, she finally succeeded. When a priest arrived she told him she would later give him evidence that Burton wanted to receive the final Catholic sacrament, and she insisted that he was still alive. Dutifully, the priest performed the sacrament. She then had Burton officially listed as a Catholic and arranged an elaborate Catholic funeral.

Isabel then spent sixteen days going through her husband's papers, journals, notebooks, manuscripts, and letters, burning many of them. Burton had probably kept detailed records of his complicated political missions as an army officer and as a diplomat that the British government would not have wanted to become public. More than that, Isabel disapproved of his interest in the sexual practices of the people he studied, and it is assumed that she burned most of these notes.

The tragedy is that, like a modern well-trained anthropologist,

ONE THOUSAND AND ONE NIGHTS

The Arabian Nights is a medieval collection of folk tales composed in Arabic and told by the beautiful Shahrazad. She was married to King Shahryar, who killed his wives after spending one night with them. He did this because he was convinced that women were deceitful. Shahrazad was able to prolong and eventually save her life by telling him a new and fascinating tale each night. In addition to being a gifted storyteller, she would sometimes either not reveal the ending until the next night or have a story continue over several nights. The king was so delighted by her tales that he spared her so she could tell a new one the next night. This pattern went on for 1,001 nights, by which time the king no longer thought of killing her. Some of Shahrazad's dramatic tales are well known today, including "Aladdin and His Magic Lamp" and "Ali Baba and the Forty Thieves."

This color engraving shows the crafty storyteller Shahrazad being seized by King Shahryar. Burton's translation of The Arabian Nights helped introduce this literary classic to an entirely new audience.

Knighted for his services to the crown, Sir Richard Francis Burton died in October 1890 after a life of adventure and study.

Burton kept meticulous daily records of whatever he considered important. Much of this information would be of great interest today. So, when it became public knowledge that she had burned these documents, the public openly condemned her and many old friends never spoke to her again.

Against Burton's family's wishes and his Protestant faith, Isabel arranged a second Catholic funeral in England and had him interred in a Catholic cemetery in a marble tomb carved in the shape of an Arab tent. In 1893 she published a biography of Burton that exceeded one thousand pages in which she presented Burton as she wanted him to be, conveniently leaving out anything that the nineteenth century would deem scandalous.

Afterword

Richard Burton's life of adventure and wide-ranging travels still captures the imaginations of many people. At a time when much of the world and many of its people were unknown to Westerners, he made a large part of it all seem familiar and exciting. In his books about South Asia, the Middle East, Africa, and South America, he brought to life places and people that were totally foreign to the English. Sometimes he shocked a conservative Christian world with his sympathetic views of other religions, especially Islam, and his curiosity about sexual practices. In these interests and concerns, he was far ahead of his time. Today the tightly clothed and stiff-lipped Victorians are often viewed as more curious than the sophisticated Muslim, African, and Indian technocrats who now live and travel throughout the world.

Burton's writings remain valuable to historians, political analysts, scholars of religion, anthropologists, and thoughtful readers everywhere.

Richard Francis Burton left a rich legacy. His groundbreaking work shed new light on unknown, overlooked, and misunderstood cultures.

His translations of Asian classics also helped open Western eyes to the riches of world literature.

Due to his physical courage and stamina, as well as his formidable knowledge of almost thirty major languages, Burton was also a major player in the Great Game. He was a faithful and useful servant of the British empire. Despite the restrictive and insensitive policies colonialism often created, his curiosity and lack of cultural bias anticipated the multicultural world we live in today.

Richard Francis Burton and His Times

1821   Richard Francis Burton is born in England on March 19.

1842   He sails to India as an officer in the army of the East India Company.

1853   He explores Arabia and visits the holy city of Mecca.

1856–1858   Burton searches for the source of the Nile River and discovers Lake Tanganyika.

1860   He travels across the United States studying the Mormons and the native tribes along the way.

1861   He assumes his first diplomatic position, as consul to Fernando Po, an island off the western coast of Africa.

1863   Burton serves as commissioner to Dahomey.

1864   He is named consul at Santos in Brazil.

1869   Burton serves as consul to Damascus, Syria.

1872–1875 He is appointed consul to Trieste.

1883   Burton's health begins to decline.

1885   He publishes his translation of *The Arabian Nights.*

1885   In recognition of his services to the British government, he is knighted.

1890   Burton dies on the morning of October 20.

Further Research

Books

Burton, Richard. *Personal Narrative of a Pilgrimage to El-Madinah and Meccah.* New York: G. P. Putnam & Co., 1856.

———. *The Lake Regions of Central Africa: A Picture of Exploration.* New York: Horizon Press, 1961.

Farwell, Byron. *Burton: A Biography of Sir Richard Francis Burton.* New York: Penguin, 1990.

Moorehead, Alan. *The White Nile.* Rev. ed. New York: Harper & Row, 1971.

Rice, Edward. *Captain Sir Richard Francis Burton: A Biography.* Cambridge, MA: Da Capo Press, 2001.

Web Sites

Drexel University, Hagerty Library, The Sir Richard Burton Society
http://www.pages.drexel.edu/~garsonkw/biography.html

Sir Richard F. Burton on the Web
http://www.isidore-of-seville.com/burton/

African Lakes
http://www.ilec.or.jp

The Nile River
http://www.nilebasin.org

The British Empire
http://www.britishempire.co.uk

BIBLIOGRAPHY

Brodie, Fawn M. *The Devil Drives: A Life of Sir Richard Burton.* New York: W. W. Norton, 1967.

Burton, Isabel. *The Life of Captain Sir Richard F. Burton.* 2 vols. New York: D. Appleton, 1893.

Burton, Richard. *Personal Narrative of a Pilgrimage to El-Madinah and Meccah.* New York: G. P. Putnam, 1856.

———. *The Lake Regions of Central Africa: A Picture of Exploration.* New York: Horizon Press, 1961.

———. *Goa, And the Blue Mountains: Or, Six Months of Sick Leave.* Santa Barbara, CA: The Narrative Press, 2001.

Farwell, Byron. *Burton: A Biography of Sir Richard Francis Burton.* New York: Penguin, 1990.

Moorehead, Alan. *The White Nile.* Rev. ed. New York: Harper & Row, 1971.

Ondaatje, Christopher. *Journey to the Source of the Nile.* Toronto, Canada: Firefly Books, 1999.

Rice, Edward. *Captain Sir Richard Francis Burton: A Biography.* Cambridge, MA: Da Capo Press, 2001.

Speke, John Hanning. *Journal of the Discovery of the Source of the Nile.* Mineola, NY: Dover Publications, 1996.

Source Notes

Chapter 3:

p. 24: "The Portuguese, it must be . . . ." Richard Burton, *Goa, and the Blue Mountains: Or, Six Months of Sick Leave.* (Santa Barbara, CA: The Narrative Press, 2001), p. 107.

Chapter 7:

p. 50: "We halted for a few minutes . . ." Richard Burton, *The Lake Regions of Central Africa: A Picture of Exploration.* Vol. 2. (New York: Horizon Press, 1961) pp. 42–43.

INDEX

Page numbers in **boldface** are illustrations.

Index